IMAGES
of Aviation
US Airways

The US Airways heritage logo, designed by employee Rusty Falk, was inspired by chairman of the board Doug Parker's desire to pay tribute to the four largest airlines that make up the new US Airways. The heritage logo is painted to the right of the main passenger entry door on all US Airways aircraft. (Courtesy US Airways Archives.)

ON THE COVER: All American Airways president Robert Love (far right) checks his watch before the company's first revenue passenger flight at Washington National Airport on March 7, 1949. Shown at left are first officer Frank Petee, chief pilot Norm Rintoul, and Capt. Tom Kincheloe. (Courtesy US Airways Archives.)

IMAGES
of Aviation

US AIRWAYS

William Lehman

ARCADIA
PUBLISHING

Published by Arcadia Publishing
Charleston, South Carolina

Printed in the United States of America

Library of Congress Control Number: 2012954442

For all general information, please contact Arcadia Publishing:
Telephone 843-853-2070
Fax 843-853-0044
E-mail sales@arcadiapublishing.com
For customer service and orders:
Toll-Free 1-888-313-2665

Visit us on the Internet at www.arcadiapublishing.com

This book is a tribute to all past employees of Allegheny, Lake Central, Mohawk, PSA, Piedmont, Empire, America West, Trump Shuttle, and MetroJet, and present employees of US Airways.

This book is dedicated to my wife, Terri, as it would have been impossible to publish these works without her love and support.

CONTENTS

ACKNOWLEDGMENTS

In late 2005, I was offered and accepted the role as volunteer corporate historian for US Airways. I have spent thousands of hours researching the history of the airline, including reviewing annual reports, employee newsletters, press releases, and notes from various board of directors meetings. I have spoken with employees to gain firsthand knowledge of the experience of working for one of the many airlines that make up today's US Airways. In addition, I have personally combed through thousands of slides and pictures from US Airways Archives to find the best images possible for this book. I have noted when photographic images were obtained from other sources.

I would like to thank Elise Eberwein, executive vice president, US Airways; John McDonald, vice president, corporate communications, US Airways; America West founders Ed and Mary Ellen Beauvais; Maurice Azurdia; Wally Bohl; Capt. Steve Gay; Joe McCarthy; Ron Peel; Jay Selman; Robert Reed, curator, Piedmont Aviation Historical Society; and Arcadia publisher Jeff Ruetsche.

—Bill Lehman
Phoenix, Arizona

One

ALLEGHENY AIRLINES

Allegheny was founded on March 5, 1937, by Richard C. DuPont, of the DuPont Chemical Company family, who hoped to contract the US Post Office to carry airmail. DuPont enlisted the help of inventor Dr. Lytle S. Adams, who, along with All American Aviation's first pilot, Norm Rintoul, studied the technology railroads used in the 19th century for dropping off and picking up mail from moving trains. Based on input from Adams and Rintoul, All American engineers crafted a unique tail-hook that hung beneath the aircraft to pick up the cloth mailbags. On March 12, 1939, All American began airmail service. The board of directors decided in 1948 that All American Aviation should change its name to All American Airways to reflect its passenger airline service. On March 7, 1949, using a Douglas DC-3, All American's first passenger flight took off from Washington National. Its destination was Pittsburgh, via several other smaller communities.

On January 1, 1953, the board of directors changed All American Airlines' name to Allegheny Airlines. As the 1950s marched on, Allegheny added more DC-3s, and it introduced Martin 202 flights in 1955. In 1959, Allegheny added its first turboprop aircraft, the Convair 540, allowing the DC-3s to be retired by 1964. Allegheny placed into service on June 1, 1965, its first Convair 580, which was a new turboprop engine from Allison for converted Convair 340 and Convair 440 aircraft. In the fall, new Fairchild F-27 turboprops were also introduced. In 1966, Allegheny placed its first jet, a DC-9-14, into service; eventually, Allegheny would operate more than 75 of the popular twin-jets. In September 1967, the last of the piston-powered aircraft, a Convair 440, was retired. Allegheny Airlines' first merger occurred on March 14, 1968, with Lake Central Airlines. With this move, Allegheny was able to further expand its route system and pick up important new cities in Indiana, Missouri, and Illinois, while adding additional Convair 580s and the French-built Nord 262 aircraft. The Nord 262s would become a huge headache for Allegheny operations and maintenance personnel due to continuous issues with the turboprop engines, which proved to be unreliable. Eventually, the engines were converted to Pratt & Whitney PT-6 turboprop engines.

On November 15, 1967, Henson Airlines became the first Allegheny Commuter Airline. Allegheny's second merger, with financially troubled Mohawk Airlines, was completed on April 12, 1972. The merger brought to Allegheny the larger Fairchild Hiller FH-227 turboprop and the British-built BAC One-Eleven. Allegheny executive Ed Colodny would assume the role of president in 1973. In line with Colodny's growth strategy, additional DC-9-30s were purchased. By 1976, the Allegheny Commuter network had grown to 12 airlines, feeding traffic to Allegheny and, in many cases, providing smaller cities with the only air service and airline they could support. Allegheny phased out the Convair 580 in 1978, although the craft continued to serve the airline well in the smaller cities as part of the Allegheny Commuter fleet. Colodny worked with presidents of the smaller airlines to pressure the Carter administration to end the monopoly held in several cities by the larger trunk airlines. In response, Congress and the Carter administration looked closely at San Diego–based Pacific Southwest Airlines (PSA) as a justification for deregulation, and by 1977, Pres. Jimmy Carter signed the Deregulation Act.

After receiving board approval, Colodny announced that Allegheny Airlines would become US Air on October 28, 1979. The new US Air would retain the Allegheny paint scheme, and the new name would be placed on the upper forward fuselage and tail.

An All American
Aviation Stinson
Reliant awaits
its first flight
on March 12,
1939, after being
awarded US Mail
route A.M. 49,
covering routes
1001 and 1002,
which linked
54 cities in
Pennsylvania, West
Virginia, Ohio,
and Delaware.

The All American
Aviation Stinson
Reliants were
equipped with a
unique tail-hook, that
hung beneath the
aircraft and allowed
the plane to pick
up cloth mailbags
without landing.

In early 1946, All
American Aviation
purchased a pair
of twin-engine
Beechcraft Beech
18s to increase
postal capacity
on denser routes
and allow pilots
to gain valuable
experience in
operating twin-
engine aircraft.

In January 1949, All American Airways was issued a three-year temporary certificate by the Civil Aeronautics Board (CAB) to carry passengers as a local service airline. All American's first Douglas DC-3 is seen undergoing pilot training flights in preparation for the first flight, which would take place on March 7, 1949.

In April 1949, All American Airways bought the assets of Salisbury, Maryland–based Chesapeake Airways for $50,000. Chesapeake had been unable to gain any additional route authority from the CAB.

On January 1, 1953, All American Airways officially became Allegheny Airlines. The new name reflected the geography covered by the airline. These two timetables reflect the name change.

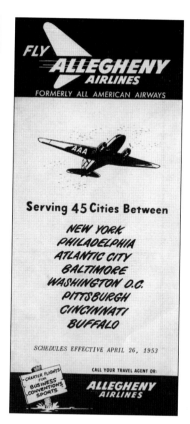

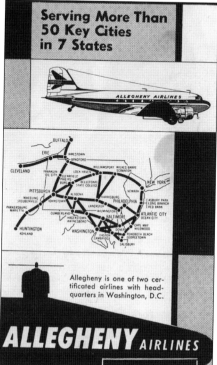

This route map reflects Allegheny Airlines' early success, due to a route system centered on heavy industry and the East Coast, which was the most densely populated region of the United States.

On April 1, 1953, a group of businessmen at Washington National Airport prepares to board an Allegheny Airlines DC-3 flight to Altoona.

A ramp agent loads an Allegheny DC-3 at Johnston, Pennsylvania, for a short hop to Pittsburgh on a late afternoon in May 1955.

Allegheny Airlines needed an aircraft that could fly farther than its DC-3s. At the same time, two airlines, California Central and Pioneer Airlines, put up for sale several used Martin 202 aircraft. Acquiring the Martin 202s became the focus of Allegheny's expansion plans. This Martin 202, called the "Martin Executive," is shown landing at Washington National Airport in the fall of 1956.

Seeing the need to update Allegheny's image, the board of directors changed the corporate logo from the green boomerang to the red and blue speed wedge, as seen on this DC-3 at Pittsburgh. The speed wedge logo would last until 1974. At the same time, the operations and maintenance base was moved from Washington National to Pittsburgh.

The Napier Engine Company offered a conversion kit to change piston-powered Convair 340s and 440s to turbo-powered aircraft called the Convair 540. Unfortunately, after five Allegheny aircraft were converted, Rolls-Royce bought Napier Engine and closed down the conversion program. This Convair 540, seen at Washington National on July 1, 1959, was the second aircraft to undergo the conversion.

Allegheny president Les Barnes, wanting to add the charm of the Hawaiian Islands to Allegheny Airlines, added seven guest hostesses from Hawaii to operate "Leilani Flights" during the summer of 1959.

An Allegheny Airlines Convair 440 is getting ready to take off on a warm summer afternoon in 1962.

The Fairchild F-27 was one of three turboprop aircraft flown by Allegheny Airlines. The F-27 would become very popular with passengers due to the large, oval windows. This aircraft is departing Philadelphia in early 1966.

Allegheny Airlines knew that the jet age had arrived for local service carriers. Bonanza Airlines was not ready to take delivery of its first Douglas DC-9-14 aircraft, so the plane was immediately leased for one year to Allegheny on July 1, 1966.

Pres. Les Barnes realized that many smaller cities were not large enough for Allegheny's fleet of turboprops and jets and tasked Vice Pres. Ed Colodny to work with the CAB. Allegheny received approval to set up marketing agreements with several smaller airlines that included one-stop check-in and seamless travel. Henson Airlines, using Beech 99s, was the first airline to become Allegheny Commuter, shown here with an Allegheny DC-9 in Pittsburgh on November 15, 1967.

Upon the merger with Lake Central Airlines, which was finalized on July 1, 1968, Allegheny inherited a new aircraft, the Nord 262, which was renamed the Mohawk 298. Allegheny repainted nine of the 12 Mohawk 298s in a purple and gold scheme and named them after stewardesses. The flights targeted prime business markets.

Chairman Henry Satterwhite and Pres. Les Barnes flew to Paris and personally interviewed Air France hostesses who were loaned to Allegheny for six months. Pictured here during a flight over Pennsylvania are an Allegheny stewardess and an Air France hostess in special French-style uniforms.

On May 27, 1969, a milestone was reached as the 500th McDonnell Douglas DC-9 built for airlines was delivered to Allegheny Airlines.

By mid-1970, Allegheny had purchased two new Boeing 727-200 aircraft to add capacity to the fleet. However, with the needed addition of a flight engineer and the high cost of maintaining these two aircraft, Allegheny sold the tri-jets to Braniff International. Allegheny had decided to stay with the DC-9. This Boeing 727-200 is seen flying over the Cascades on April 1, 1970, just before Allegheny accepted delivery of the new jet.

During a warm summer day in 1973, two Allegheny BAC One-Elevens sit between flights in Pittsburgh. Allegheny inherited the BAC One-Elevens from the merger with Mohawk Airlines.

First officer Vince Lo Prinzi (left), Capt. Ernie Mast (second from left), and stewardess Diane Gushi (far right) pause between flights to talk with an unidentified passenger in front of an Allegheny Convair 580.

A new look premiered with a new aircraft, the McDonnell Douglas DC-9-50, shown here during a pilot training flight over Pennsylvania in October 1975. The new aircraft provided increased capacity while keeping costs down, since it was simply a stretch of the DC-9-30 aircraft. However, hot summer temperatures severely weight-restricted the aircraft. Allegheny traded the DC-9-50s with Eastern Airlines' smaller DC-9-30s, a transaction that was completed by November 1978.

Pittsburgh, shown here during a busy afternoon in the fall of 1978, continued to be the number-one hub for Allegheny. Allegheny had learned years earlier about the benefit of feeding traffic through a hub-and-spoke network.

In December 1978, an Allegheny BAC One-Eleven taxis toward the runway at Washington National for an afternoon flight to Pittsburgh. (Photograph by Jay Selman.)

In early 1978, as United Airlines started parking older Boeing 727-100s, Pres. Ed Colodny moved quickly to acquire the 11 aircraft and placed them into service.

In September 1979, this Allegheny DC-9-30 taxis toward the gate at Washington National Airport following a morning flight from Philadelphia. (Photograph by Jay Selman.)

Pres. Ed Colodny received approval from the board of directors to change the name from Allegheny to US Air, effective October 28, 1979. Colodny wanted the name changed to reflect the new US Air's focus on adding flights to the Midwest and West Coast. This is the first DC-9-30 painted with the new name. Allegheny's three stripes (red, burgundy, and maroon) were maintained.

Two

Lake Central Airlines

In 1940, aviation pioneer, air racer, and decorated World War I hero Roscoe Turner and two other partners founded Roscoe Turner Aeronautical Corporation (RTAC). Once the United States was involved in World War II, Turner was awarded a contract to teach basic air training to Army students. In 1947, RTAC applied to the Civil Aeronautical Board (CAB) for authority to begin passenger service. In February 1948, the CAB issued temporary authority for RTAC to serve cities in Ohio, Indiana, Kentucky, Michigan, and Illinois as a local service carrier. RTAC decided to base its new airline in Indianapolis and rename the company Turner Airlines. Roscoe Turner would hold only a minority stake in the airline. John and Paul Weesner were the majority stockholders. Turner, however, would use his popularity and public relations skills to promote the airline in the new cities to be served. Turner Airlines officially launched service on November 12, 1949. In November 1950, Turner Airlines became Lake Central Airlines. In 1952, Roscoe Turner sold his 25-percent stake in Lake Central to the Weesner brothers, and in turn, the Weesners decided to sell the company.

By the end of 1952, Lake Central phased out the Beech Bonanzas. Dr. R.B. Stewart became chairman of the board and president of Lake Central in 1953, and he immediately embarked on major changes to improve the struggling airline, including changes in several key management positions. He ordered new interiors for the DC-3s, which were now called Centraliners. Lake Central developed important feeder connections with the major airlines, and by the end of the year, many of its passengers were transferring to or from the majors. This greatly increased the profitability of the routes that were flown. Lake Central was an early industry leader in quick turns at the smaller stations, accomplished by leaving the right engine running while passengers, baggage, freight, and mail were unloaded and loaded. The DC-3s averaged four-minute turns, allowing Lake Central to operate its entire route system with just seven DC-3s.

In 1959, Lake Central employees' stock went from a trust directly to the employees. Employee morale and pride were at an all-time high. In 1960, as Lake Central continued to expand, additional capital needed to be raised, and the employees voted to have a public stock issuance. While this raised critical cash for Lake Central, it would signal the end of employee ownership. As Lake Central was now a public company, the board of directors called for a new, bold corporate identity. In 1961, new Convair 340s were purchased from United Airlines. Lake Central called these planes "the radar Convairs" to promote safety, as these were the first weather-radar-equipped aircraft. Lake Central was also able to purchase 10 additional DC-3s. While 1962 and 1963 were relatively quiet years for Lake Central, the airline was earning an industry-wide reputation for being the friendliest air carrier in the Midwest. During this time, the route map continued to expand, with an extensive schedule operating throughout the Midwest. Late in 1963, Pres. Lloyd Hartman started a search for a replacement aircraft for the DC-3. Hartman, one of the former vice presidents brought into the airline during the North Central merger attempt by former Lake

Central president Stewart, soon had the respect of the employees and board of directors and was named president.

In 1966, after less than a year in service, the Nord 262 aircraft were already becoming a big headache for Lake Central. The Turbomeca Bastan turboprop engines were called "turbo-bastards" by pilots and mechanics. Constant mechanical delays and cancellations were costing the airline passengers, as reliability was quickly slipping. Within six weeks, three engines on three different aircraft disintegrated during flight. Lake Central had no choice but to ground the entire fleet, while putting back into service several DC-3s that had been retired. As 1966 came to a close, Lake Central management was at odds with the French manufacturer, demanding an immediate fix for the grounded Nords. Lake Central moved forward with a conversion program to modify the piston-driven Convair 340s with Allison-powered turboprops called Convair 580s. In early 1967, engineers in France found that the problem was with water methanol (used to boost power at takeoff) and mineral corrosion. This was the root cause of the engine disintegration problem. By February 1967, the Nord 262s returned to the skies, and President Hartman flew to Seattle and negotiated with Boeing for three brand-new Boeing 737-200s, with first delivery to occur a year later. The last DC-3 was retired from Lake Central on October 27, 1967.

On March 12, 1968, the merger of Lake Central Airlines and Allegheny Airlines was approved by both companies' boards of directors. It was decided that Allegheny Airlines would be the surviving name, since Allegheny had controlling interest. The merger was completed on July 1, 1968.

One of Turner Airlines' pilots prepares the aircraft for takeoff, while one of the Weesner brothers—who held controlling interest and 75 percent of the stock in Roscoe Turner's new airline—loads mail into a Beech Bonanza on November 10, 1949. The aircraft was painted dark blue and red, with additional "Lake Central Routes" written on both sides of the fuselage.

A Turner Airlines DC-3 sits on the ramp at Indianapolis with a lone stewardess ready to receive passengers. This photograph was taken on the first day of service, November 12, 1949.

Passengers and Turner Airline executives pause for the camera before boarding the first multi-stop flight from Grand Rapids to Indianapolis on November 12, 1949.

Turner Airlines DC-3s and Beech Bonanzas sit on the ramp in Indianapolis at the end of November 1949. While Turner Airlines highly publicized the DC-3s, over half of the cities were served using the Bonanzas. Many of the smaller cities' runways were too short for the DC-3s, which forced Turner to use the three-seat Bonanzas, which was also an early indication that certain towns were extremely limited in their capacity to handle lots of passengers.

In January 1955, the Weesners sold their Lake Central stock shares to the employees. While the stock was held in trust, Lake Central became America's first "employee owned" airline. This became a great marketing tool that appeared on timetables and billboards. In this photograph from the early fall of 1960, a Lake Central pilot and station agent review paperwork at the Marion, Ohio, ticket counter.

In 1960, Lake Central employees voted to have a public stock issuance, which would signal the end of employee ownership. The public stock issuance was a success for Lake Central, which needed to find larger aircraft. United Airlines had a huge fleet of 44-seat Convair 340s that were ready to be phased out. Because Lake Central now had much-needed cash, Dr. R.B. Stewart, who was both chairman of the board and president, immediately purchased 10 Convair 340s, placing the first aircraft into service in October 1960. This Convair 340 is seen returning to Indianapolis from Cincinnati on March 1, 1961.

This Lake Central DC-3 looks smart with its red-and-blue-striped paint scheme as it flies from Youngstown to Columbus on April 30, 1962. Lake Central came up with a brilliant marketing scheme during this time, offering DC-3 promotional flights on Saturdays, when those aircraft would normally be parked. This allowed Lake Central to carry passengers who otherwise might not have flown and helped generate loyal customers for the airline.

In March 1964, Lake Central president Lloyd Hartman signed a contract to buy eight French-made Nord 262 turboprops. The 27-seat aircraft, with its high wing and large, oval windows, was seen as a perfect replacement for the DC-3. Lake Central held an open house at Indianapolis in early April 1965 to introduce the media, travel agents, and potential passengers to the Nord 262. The Convair 240 and DC-3 were also showcased.

In this October 1, 1965, photograph, a Lake Central Nord 262 is seen boarding passengers for a flight from Indianapolis to Bloomington, while the DC-3 in the background is operating a five-stop flight to Buffalo.

In the October 1965 photograph below, Lake Central stewardess Caren Cartnell shows off the interior of the new Nord 262 at Lake Central's home base of Indianapolis.

Flying over Indiana on August 11, 1966, was the first Lake Central Convair 580 delivered by Allison Division of General Motors. Eventually, all of Lake Central's former piston-powered Convair 340s would be converted.

In June 1967, Lloyd Hartman was ousted by the board of directors and replaced with Thomas Ferguson, who had worked for Allegheny Airlines. Ferguson felt that the marketing theme was outdated, and he immediately began a new campaign, called "airline with a heart." He mandated that the tails of Lake Central aircraft be painted red, with a white heart in the middle, as seen on this Convair 580.

Lake Central continued to promote the new marketing theme on billboards, ticket counters, gates, and schedules, as seen in this timetable from early 1968.

Lake Central's advertising department printed thousands of "Love at First Flight" stickers, which were given to employees, travel agents, and passengers. These stickers were handed out in the fall of 1967.

Maintenance issues associated with the Nord 262 Turbomeca Bastan engines caused a complete grounding of the fleet for a few months. In response, the marketing department turned its attention to promoting the Convair 580, as seen on this pamphlet handed out to the traveling public in late 1966.

Lake Central executives congratulate Glen L. Schwartz (center) on becoming the airline's five-millionth passenger on October 6, 1967. Lake Central announced a few days later that the board of directors was in merger talks with Allegheny Airlines.

On July 1, 1968, Lake Central formally merged with Allegheny Airlines. Below, executives of both Lake Central and Allegheny cut into a cake delivered by American Airlines to celebrate the first day of combined operations under the Allegheny Airlines name.

Three

MOHAWK AIRLINES

In 1945, C.S. Robinson founded Robinson Aviation, which was awarded government contracts to perform aerial photography using a Fairchild F-24 aircraft equipped with cameras mounted through floor panels. Robinson Aviation's first passenger flight occurred on April 6, 1945. As 1946 began, Robinson Aviation retired the F-24s and T-50s and replaced the aircraft with Beechcraft D-18s. Robinson decided on the Beech 18 because the aircraft carried double the passengers of the aircraft used before. Robinson Aviation was renamed Robinson Airlines, and the company started advertising itself as "Route of the Air Chiefs." In Ithaca, Robinson called upon a large farmers' cooperative to invest in the new company, since they were equally concerned with establishing a solid air transportation network out of their community. With financing in place, Robinson submitted his formal application to the Civil Aeronautics Board. The airline purchased three used DC-3s, painting them white with an air chief logo in red and blue on the tail and a red stripe running under the windows. The CAB awarded Robinson Airlines a three-year temporary certificate in February 1948.

In early 1952, C.S. Robinson removed himself from the day-to-day operations of the airline. Following this change, the board of directors, for the last time, renamed the company Mohawk Airlines. In addition, Mohawk was given a permanent certificate to operate as a local service carrier. In 1954, Robert Peach became president of Mohawk Airlines. On July 1, 1955, Mohawk inaugurated "Cosmopolitan" Convair 240 service and continued to be a leader by being the first local service carrier to offer aircraft with pressurization. Mohawk found that the Convair 240 "Air Chiefs" had much greater range than the DC-3s. Because of this improved flight range, Mohawk applied for and was granted additional routes to Detroit, Michigan, and Erie, Pennsylvania. As 1956 dawned, because of the growing number of aircraft in the Mohawk fleet, the hangar in Ithaca had become obsolete. Peach went to both Ithaca and Utica to try to work out the best arrangement for new facilities. Within a short time, he signed a long-term lease with Utica to build both a new hangar and corporate offices for Mohawk. In the summer of 1959, Mohawk became the first local service carrier to introduce the new Convair 440 Metropolitan, and in 1961, Mohawk became the first US airline to centralize its reservation system.

Peach announced Mohawk's first pure jet purchase of four new British-made BAC One-Elevens in July 1962, followed by an order for 18 Fairchild Hiller FH-227 turboprop aircraft that would fly into cities unable to support the BAC One-Elevens. Mohawk placed these orders with the plan to start aggressively retiring the Convair 240s and 440s. In late 1964, Mohawk opened its new corporate headquarters in Utica. Mohawk's first BAC One-Eleven did a low flyby over Utica on May 17, 1965, to announce that the jet age had arrived. By the end of 1965, Mohawk became the first local service carrier to open and operate flight simulators for both the BAC One-Elevens and Fairchild Hiller FH-227s. In January 1969, Mohawk moved into the new reservation center and switched to a new system called Direct Airlines Reservation and Ticketing. Robert Peach was named CEO and board chairman to focus on the financial problems facing the airline, while Russell V. Stevenson was named president and was immediately tasked with running the day-to-day operations.

In early 1970, Peach stepped down from his position as chairman and CEO, although he remained a member of the board of directors. Mohawk could no longer afford to continue to operate the BAC One-Elevens and Fairchild Hiller FH-227s into smaller cities and decided to copy rival Allegheny Airlines in creating a network, called the Mohawk Commuter Network. In 1971, with Mohawk in poor financial shape, Stevenson went to lending institutions but was rejected. He then went directly to Allegheny Airlines for help. Allegheny's board of directors made an offer to Mohawk's board. The offer consisted of Allegheny Airlines stock, as the board would not spend any cash to merge Mohawk into its own operations. No key management from Mohawk would transition to Allegheny. Only the aircraft, along with most of the frontline employees, would migrate to the merged airline. Robert Peach, who had been the key person in building and running Mohawk since the beginning, could not bear to watch his airline disappear. He walked out of the boardroom before the Mohawk board of directors took the final vote. He resigned one week later and, less than two weeks after that, he ended his own life. The merger was completed on April 12, 1972, as Mohawk became Allegheny Airlines.

In 1945, C.S. Robinson founded Robinson Aviation. Shown here are, from left to right, William Corcoran, Ralph Smith, Leo Cass, B.M. Clarey, Gertrude Grover, C.S. Robinson, and Capt. Al Eager. They are standing in front of the airline's Fairchild F-24 on the day of the first scheduled flight on April 6, 1945, between Ithaca and Flushing.

Shown in Ithaca in the fall of 1945 are both of Robinson Aviation's three-seat Fairchild F-24s. C.S. Robinson had picked Ithaca as the home base for his airline because rail service was non-existent and the roads were in poor condition, making driving difficult.

In February 1948, Robinson Airlines was awarded a three-year temporary certificate to operate as a local service carrier. An open house was held that same month to showcase each aircraft Robinson had flown from 1945 to 1948, including, from left to right, the Fairchild F-24, Cessna T-50, Beechcraft D-18, and Robinson's first Douglas DC-3.

Shown with other original Robinson Airlines employees is Robert Peach (far right), who had been hired as the third pilot at Robinson and was named general manager in late February 1948. Robinson Airlines was now predominately serving cities in what was known as the Mohawk Valley.

In early 1952, with C.S. Robinson removing himself from day-to-day operations, the board of directors formally changed the name to Mohawk Airlines. A permanent certificate was granted to Mohawk to operate as a local service carrier. Shown here in August 1952 is one of Mohawk's Douglas DC-3s.

Lynn Smith is shown in May 1955 poking his head out of the first officer's window of Mohawk Airlines' first Convair 240. Smith, an Onondaga Indian, was hired by Mohawk's marketing department as a living mascot during the summer of 1953. Known as "Little Mo," Lynn would appear in newspaper, radio, and television advertisements. Little Mo became so popular that Pres. Robert Peach had him make personal appearances throughout the route system promoting Mohawk Airlines.

On June 7, 1954, Mohawk became the first local service carrier to offer helicopter passage. The route went between Newark, New Jersey, and Grossinger Field in New York using this Sikorsky S-55. The service would only last the summer before being discontinued due to the high costs of running the helicopter.

On the cold morning of December 13, 1956, two Mohawk DC-3s and one Convair 240 sit idle at Ithaca. Mohawk's fleet of 11 DC-3s and 13 Convair 240s had outgrown the hangar.

A Mohawk Convair 240 flies between Ithaca and Syracuse in the spring of 1957. Peach decided that Mohawk needed to bump up capacity on the Convair 240s, so he had maintenance personnel install six additional seats by removing a galley and main deck cargo bin, bringing the passenger capacity to 46 seats.

Since a passenger's first impression of an airline was the ticket counter, Peach ensured that every Mohawk Airlines check-in counter looked professional, as seen here at Utica in late 1959.

Standing in front of one of Mohawk's Convair 240s are first officer Harold "Skippy" Van Valkenburg (left) and two unidentified Mohawk employees. Skippy's daughter, Cindy Newton, is a flight attendant with US Airways today.

In September 1960, Peach introduced the "Gas Light Service," flying DC-3s from Buffalo to Rochester, Syracuse, and Boston. As shown here, the DC-3s were fitted with a special paint scheme of red and white, with "Mohawk Gas Light Service" written on the side of the aircraft and a red, white, yellow, and black gas lantern on the tail. Although this had been intended as a short-term publicity stunt by Mohawk's marketing department, the unique flights would last almost two years.

The interiors of the special DC-3s were decorated with Victorian-style red velvet curtains, carriage lamps, and decorated seats, while the lone stewardess wore a "gas light" costume. Free beer was served in large steins along with cheese and pretzels, as well as 5¢ cigars. When the service began, only men were allowed to fly on these aircraft. Following public pressure, however, Mohawk gave in and allowed women and children to travel in a newly designed family parlor, which was still divided by a curtain from the men.

40

With many unsold 440s sitting at Convair's San Diego plant, Mohawk jumped at the opportunity to purchase the new aircraft at a reasonable rate. With the introduction of the new Convairs, Mohawk rolled out a new paint scheme consisting of gold and black stripes that ran the length of the fuselage. Pictured here is Mohawk's first Convair 440 at Utica in November 1961.

On a cool spring morning in 1963, this Martin 404 taxis for takeoff out of Ithaca for a quick flight to Syracuse. Peach found that the Martin 404 was not a good fit for Mohawk's large Convair fleet. He contacted Ozark Airlines and worked out an exchange whereby the Mohawk Martin 404s would be traded for Ozark's Convair 240s. This deal was completed by the end of 1965.

On May 16, 1965, Peach (left) was in England to pick up Mohawk's first BAC One-Eleven. England's Prince Philip (front right) was on hand to congratulate Mohawk on being the first airline to put the twin-jet into service in the United States. After a short speech, Peach hopped on the new airplane for the trip across the Atlantic.

On May 17, 1965, employees viewed Mohawk's first BAC One-Eleven in Utica. While Peach had expected only a few hundred people to show up, thousands came out to tour the airline's first jet aircraft. It was placed into service on July 11, 1965.

In May 1966, Mohawk's chairman of the board, E. Victor Underwood, dedicated the first Fairchild Hiller FH-227. The "227 Prop Jet," with its large, oval windows and high wing design, became very popular with passengers when it was placed into service in June 1966.

During a summer day in 1968, a Fairchild Hiller FH-227 takes off from Utica for Hartford. The Rolls-Royce Dart engines were equipped with water methanol to boost takeoff performance on hot, humid days.

In early 1969, a Mohawk BAC One-Eleven is shown en route to New York City. While Mohawk was a much smaller airline than its rivals, the friendly spirit of its employees was well known.

Peach flew to Seattle to order three new Boeing 727-200s, planned for a late 1969 delivery. The aircraft shown here in Mohawk livery is a touched-up photograph provided by Boeing's marketing department. Much to Peach's surprise, the larger trunk airlines, placed political pressure on the CAB, successfully blocked Mohawk from getting coast-to-coast routes. The Boeing 727-200s were too large for Mohawk's existing routes, and Peach was forced to cancel the order. The planes would be resold to PSA.

On May 1, 1969, a newly graduated class of Mohawk stewardesses stands behind a model of a Boeing 737. After the cancellation of the Boeing 727s, Peach signed an order for the smaller 737. The baby Boeing was a natural fit for many of Mohawk's existing markets, but Peach would be forced to cancel the order by early 1970, as Mohawk could not finance the purchase.

To pay tribute to the heritage of Mohawk Airlines, four BAC One-Elevens were painted in a special "buckskin" livery. Orange and tan stripes ran the length of the plane, as seen on this aircraft en route to Washington, DC, on an early afternoon in October 1969.

Four Mohawk employees wear new uniforms, which debuted in 1970. Pictured are, from left to right, stewardess Barbara Stein and Mohawk ground employees Frank Banko, Jean Fithen, and David Fowler.

Sharing the ramp at Pittsburgh on April 11, 1972, are an Allegheny Airlines DC-9-30 and a Mohawk BAC One-Eleven. One day later, the Mohawk name would disappear from the planes, as Mohawk Airlines became Allegheny.

Four

PACIFIC SOUTHWEST AIRLINES—PSA

In 1945, San Diego resident Kenny G. Friedkin founded Friedkin Aeronautics. The new company's specialty was training servicemen just returned from World War II how to fly, using a Cessna UC-78, under the government's National Rehabilitation Act. Friedkin realized that if his company was going to survive, he would need to switch gears from training pilots to starting an airline capable of carrying passengers. With very little startup capital, Friedkin found a DC-3 that was available for lease at rates he could afford. Friedkin called the DC-3 a "Luxurious Skyliner" and named his new airline Pacific Southwest Airlines, or PSA. Friedkin knew that the fitness hearings held by the Civil Aeronautics Board for prospective new airlines was a long and laborious process. Another option was needed. Friedkin turned to California's Public Utilities Commission, which would have jurisdiction over the new airline. On May 6, 1949, PSA's first flight took off from San Diego to Burbank and Oakland. In 1950, PSA recognized that sailors had weekend furloughs to visit family and friends up the coast and could now afford to fly with the low airfares being charged. In fact, so many sailors flew PSA that the airline became known as "Poor Sailors Airline."

As 1951 arrived, PSA continued its simple yet effective three-city route system. Friedkin ensured that all PSA employees had fun with the passengers and recognized that the key to success was friendly, safe, reliable, and dependable air service. In 1957, upon hearing that PSA could not finance a proposed order for the French-built Sud Caravelle jet, Lockheed brought the prototype Electra to San Diego. With Lockheed assisting in getting the necessary financing, PSA placed an order for three 98-seat Electras, with first delivery planned for late 1959. In 1958, Friedkin made sure that PSA hired the most beautiful women in California, who were then trained to pamper passengers and to use their sense of humor to entertain. PSA accepted delivery in November 1959 of the first four-engine Lockheed Electra turboprop. Since quick turnaround of aircraft was still important, stewardesses were tasked with collecting tickets onboard the aircraft. In March 1962, founder Kenny Friedkin passed away suddenly. J. Floyd "Andy" Andrews, who had started with Friedkin Aeronautics, succeeded Friedkin. On April 9, 1965, PSA entered the jet age, as the first Boeing 727-100 was delivered and placed into service, and in 1967, Andrews signed an order with Boeing for ten 737-200s. By March 1969, the Lockheed Electras were phased out.

In 1969, with the arrival of the Boeing 737s, Andrews set up two subsidiaries, Jet Air Leasing and Pacific Southwest Airmotive, the latter specializing in overhauling jet engines. In 1970, PSA decided to buy or build a hotel in every city PSA flew into. Andrews set up a new holding company, PSA, Inc., as the airline expanded into other areas, including car rental, sport fishing, and several radio stations. On Christmas Eve, Andrews announced that PSA had placed an order for two Lockheed Tri-Star L-1011 jets, while mechanic Cleve Jackson convinced Andrews to put a smile on the front of PSA aircraft. In 1971, PSA's car subsidiary, Val-car, was sold. As 1972 opened, Andrews outfitted PSA aircraft with a new paint scheme: colorful stripes of pink, red, and orange on the side of the airplane, a sweeping rooster tail on the tail, and the signature black smile on the front. In 1975, the board of directors ordered Andrews to immediately start selling off unprofitable parts of the company. Andrews announced his retirement, as many on the board felt he was to blame for PSA's financial difficulties. William Shimp became chairman and CEO, and Paul Barkley would fill the role of president.

In the fall of 1977, PSA addressed a minor problem: the pink color in the paint scheme was fading too fast under the California sun and so was changed to orange. With the introduction of the Airline Deregulation Act in 1978, PSA opened its first two interstate cities, Las Vegas and Reno. Now the 12th-largest airline in the United States, PSA turned to McDonnell Douglas's redesigned new aircraft, called the DC-9 Super 80. PSA was the US launch customer for quiet, fuel-efficient twin-jets. In the fall, PSA introduced automated ticket machines at San Francisco, Los Angeles, and San Diego. In April 1980, PSA opened its first two international cities, Puerto Vallarta and Mazatlan, both reached from Los Angeles. PSA received the first new DC-9 Super 80, known as "the world's quietest commercial jetliner," in October.

In 1981, PSA opened its multi-million-dollar pilot and flight attendant training center at Scripps Ranch. Braniff International filed for bankruptcy in May 1982 and ceased flying. PSA then worked on a reorganization plan that would have PSA flying 25 to 30 former Braniff Boeing 727s out of Dallas in PSA's paint scheme. The plan was abandoned by February 1983. PSA started assigning seats and began a new, lucrative frequent flyer program called Executive Flyer in the spring. As the year marched on, PSA started looking for smaller aircraft. British Aerospace heard of PSA's dilemma and invited the company to England to view the quad jet that promised 30 percent reduced fuel savings over the Super 80s. PSA would leave England with an order for 20. PSA moved from terminal six to terminal one in Los Angeles in January 1984. In the spring, PSA became the first US airline to order the heads-up display, or HUD, for all Super 80s, allowing PSA to operate with much lower landing minimums at several airports. During this time, Shimp became chairman of the board and Barkley became the CEO. On June 20, the first revenue flight of the BAe146, called "The Smileliner," took place between Burbank and Oakland. Major problems with the new aircraft would quickly grab PSA's attention, while conditions inside the aircraft would cause capacity to be reduced to 83 seats. PSA's last Boeing 727-200 operated the final flight between Las Vegas and San Diego on November 26, 1984.

In the early part of 1985, the company introduced the PSA Expressway, offering departures every half-hour during the week in both directions between Los Angeles and San Francisco. This was followed by the opening of a second reservation center in Reno. In May 1985, William Shimp passed away suddenly, and the board named Barkley chairman and former Eastern Airlines executive Russell Ray president. In the fall, PSA moved into a new terminal at San Francisco that included additional gates to support future expansion. In February 1986, PSA started naming all aircraft individually after cities and states that were served by the carrier. In January 1987, with a simple phone call from Washington, DC, to San Diego, PSA agreed to be acquired by US Air. US Air president Ed Colodny flew to San Diego to make the formal announcement of the merger to the media and employees. Both TWA and Northwest announced that, by the end of 1987, they would terminate the code share agreements signed a few years earlier. On April 9, 1988, PSA officially became US Air, marking the third merger in the history of the company.

In 1945, Kenny Friedkin founded Friedkin Aeronautics (above), whose focus was training returning servicemen to fly under the GI Bill.

At right, Kenny Friedkin sits at his desk in preparation for launching his new airline, Pacific Southwest Airlines, or PSA. Friedkin, knowing that the fitness hearings before the Civil Aeronautics Board was a long and laborious process, turned to the California Public Utilities Commission, who would have both economic and pricing authority over his airline.

Below, with its simple red stripe, is PSA's first leased Douglas DC-3, which Friedkin called his "Luxurious Skyliner." PSA's first flight would take off from San Diego on May 6, 1949, to Oakland via Burbank.

With very little start-up capital, Friedkin bought whatever he could get his hands on, including this converted Marine Corps outhouse, which would become PSA's first building asset. One of PSA's original customer service agents is shown here in late 1949 taking phone reservations for the airline's three-city network.

Shown here proudly wearing PSA's first uniforms, designed by PSA cofounder Jean Friedkin, are, from left to right, Capt. Bud Plosser, stewardess Ramona Tower, and copilot Major Thom.

The entire PSA fleet of four DC-3s is shown sitting in San Diego mid-week in 1952. PSA continued to stress high frequency between the cities in its route system. PSA was an early pioneer in five-minute turns between flights, as Friedkin knew that airplanes do not generate profits sitting on the ground for long periods of time.

In early 1955, PSA purchased two used 70-seat DC-4s from Capital Airlines. Friedkin was very careful not to mention that the aircraft were for PSA. He maintained Capital's red stripe and simply added "PSA" over the Capital Airlines name on the aircraft to save money, as shown here on PSA's first DC-4 flying over San Francisco in October 1956.

One of PSA's DC-4s sits on the ramp in San Diego after being retired from service in November 1960. PSA would sell all four DC-4s at a profit, much to Friedkin's surprise.

Local California Time Light Face—A.M. Bold Face—P.M.							LOS ANGELES INTERNATIONAL FLIGHTS												EFFECTIVE MARCH 18, 1960	
DAILY MONDAY THRU THURSDAY							**FRIDAY ONLY**													
Northbound	723	809	123	239	449	603	709	Northbound	723	809	119	123	259	303	501	529	643	753	759	959
Lv. San Diego	7:15	8:00	12:35	2:35	4:45	6:00		Lv. San Diego	7:15	8:00	11:00	12:35		3:00	5:00		6:45			
Ar. Los Angeles		8:25		3:00	5:10			Ar. Los Angeles		8:25	11:25									
Lv. Los Angeles		8:40		3:15	5:25		7:05	Lv. Los Angeles		8:40	11:40		2:35			5:20			7:55	9:55
Ar. Burbank	7:45		1:05			6:30		Ar. Burbank	7:45			1:00		3:30			7:15			
Lv. Burbank	8:00		1:20			6:45		Lv. Burbank	8:00			1:15		3:45			7:30	7:55		
Ar. San Francisco	8:50	9:35	2:10	4:10	6:20	7:35	8:00	Ar. San Francisco	8:50	9:35	12:35	2:10	3:30	4:35	6:10	6:15	8:20	8:45	8:50	10:50
Southbound	734	106	144	346	546	654	756	Southbound	734	106	154	156	304	406	500	646	644	846	900	956
Lv. San Francisco	7:30	10:00	1:45	3:45	5:45	6:55	7:55	Lv. San Francisco	7:30	10:00	1:00	1:15	3:00	4:00	5:00	6:40	6:45	8:45	9:10	9:25
Ar. Burbank	8:20		2:35			7:45		Ar. Burbank	8:20		1:50		3:50				7:35			
Lv. Burbank	8:35		2:50			8:00		Lv. Burbank	8:35		2:05		4:05							
Ar. Los Angeles		10:55		4:40	6:40		8:50	Ar. Los Angeles		10:55		2:10		4:55		7:35		9:40		10:20
Lv. Los Angeles		11:10		4:55			9:05	Lv. Los Angeles		11:10										10:35
Ar. San Diego	9:05	11:35	3:20	5:20		8:30	9:30	Ar. San Diego	9:05	11:35	2:35		4:35		6:10				10:20	11:00
SATURDAY ONLY								**SUNDAY ONLY**												
Northbound	723	809	109	123	239	449	603	Northbound	903	119	123	259	223	529	503	621	759	841	929	139	133	159
Lv. San Diego	7:15	8:00	10:00	12:35	2:35	4:45	6:00	Lv. San Diego	9:00	11:00	12:35		2:15		5:00	6:20		8:45				
Ar. Los Angeles		8:25	10:25		3:00	5:10		Ar. Los Angeles		11:25												
Lv. Los Angeles		8:40	10:40		3:15	5:25		Lv. Los Angeles		11:40		2:35		5:20			7:55		9:20	10:35		11:55
Ar. Burbank	7:45			1:05	.		6:30	Ar. Burbank	9:30				2:45		5:30						11:30	
Lv. Burbank	8:00			1:20			6:45	Lv. Burbank	9:45				3:00		5:45						11:30	
Ar. San Francisco	8:50	9:35	11:35	2:10	4:10	6:20	7:35	Ar. San Francisco	10:35	12:35	2:10	3:30	3:50	6:10	6:35	7:30	8:50	9:55	10:15	11:30	12:20	12:50
Southbound	734	926	114	116	344	654	756	Southbound	906	124	156	244	406	414	406	700	816	916	104	146	134
Lv. San Francisco	7:30	9:25	10:30	1:00	3:45	6:55	7:55	Lv. San Francisco	9:00	12:00	1:15	2:45	4:00	4:15	6:40	7:00	8:00	9:15	10:25	10:45	11:45	12:50
Ar. Burbank	8:20		11:20			7:45		Ar. Burbank		12:50			3:35		5:05				11:15			1:40
Lv. Burbank	8:35		11:35			8:00		Lv. Burbank		1:05			3:50		5:20							1:55
Ar. Los Angeles		10:20		1:55	4:40		8:50	Ar. Los Angeles	9:55		2:10		4:55			7:35		8:55	10:10	11:40		
Lv. Los Angeles		10:35		2:10	4:55		9:05	Lv. Los Angeles	10:10													
Ar. San Diego	9:05	11:00	12:05	2:35	5:20	8:30	9:30	Ar. San Diego	10:35	1:35		4:20		5:50		8:10					12:55	2:25
PSA Stewardesses use Fabrege perfumes and Juliette Marglen cosmetics. Carte Blanche welcomed on all Flights.								ALL FLIGHTS ELECTRA JET							**THE WORLD'S LEADING INTRA-STATE AIRLINE**						

PSA's March 18, 1960, schedule (above) shows frequent service over the airline's four-city route system. The four-engine turboprop Lockheed Electra was now the workhorse of the airline that proudly advertised being the "world's leading intra-state airline."

At left, in 1961, two PSA reservation agents are shown using old-style reservation cards to block seats on specific flights. It was simple and kept PSA's costs below those of its competitors.

In late 1962, PSA's first Lockheed Electra is seen flying over California and Nevada's Sierra Nevadas.

Lady Bird Johnson is shown deplaning in San Francisco in late 1965 having just flown from Los Angeles on a PSA chartered Boeing 727-100. PSA would become the airline of choice for stars, entertainers, and politicians.

During the summer of 1967, PSA started helicopter service between San Diego's Lindbergh Field and three area hotels. The experiment lasted only one month, as operating one helicopter became cost-prohibitive.

In the May 1968 photograph above, one of PSA's new Boeing 727-200s is seen flying over the San Fernando Mountains.

Unlike other airlines, PSA used real stewardesses for commercials, print advertisements, and ticket jackets, such as this one from the "hot pants" era in 1968.

Seen here in August 1969, flying from San Francisco to Ontario, California, is one of PSA's Boeing 737-200s. PSA would eventually operate 13 twin-jet aircraft, although the fleet would be phased out by March 1976, when PSA would operate only two aircraft types, the Boeing 727 and the Lockheed Electra.

PSA reintroduced the Lockheed Electra in 1975, a move made necessary since jet aircraft were prohibited from flying into South Lake Tahoe. PSA flight 98 to Burbank is shown at the small mountainous town on a warm summer afternoon in August 1975.

PSA's first wide-body aircraft, the Lockheed L-1011 Tri-Star, is shown landing at Los Angeles from San Francisco on the first day of service, August 1, 1974.

With the Arab oil embargo, short one-hour flights, and the L-1011's long loading and unloading times, PSA quickly discovered that it was uneconomical to continue to fly the wide-bodied aircraft. The two aircraft were parked, and the remaining orders were cancelled.

Above, PSA's Electra sits at Burbank on an October day in 1978. After failing to convince South Lake Tahoe to allow jet aircraft into the airport, the company closed the station, exited the market in 1979, and sold the four Lockheed Electras.

PSA flight attendants model new uniforms on the wing of a Boeing 727-200 in early 1980.

PSA continued to dominate all the cities served, including the very competitive Los Angeles–to–San Francisco corridor; one of PSA's Boeing 727-200s taxis toward the runway on a busy Friday afternoon in 1981. PSA would operate a total of 16 Boeing 727-100s and 34 Boeing 727-200s. (Photograph by Jay Selman.)

PSA was the US launch customer for the DC-9 Super 80, which would become the MD-80. PSA's first MD-80 is shown here flying over the California coast in the fall of 1982.

In May 1983, PSA purchased four used DC-9-30s from Air Canada for expansion into the Pacific Northwest. This DC-9 is shown landing at Las Vegas from San Francisco in December 1986. PSA operated the DC-9-30 twice in the company's history. (Photograph by Jay Selman.)

PSA's president, Paul Barkley, ordered 20 with options to purchase 20 more British Aerospace BAe146-200s. The aircraft would become a major headache for PSA mechanics and the airline. PSA's BAe146s were breaking down so often that British Aerospace loaned three BAe146-100s at various times to act as backup aircraft in an attempt to raise aircraft reliability. (Photograph by Jay Selman.)

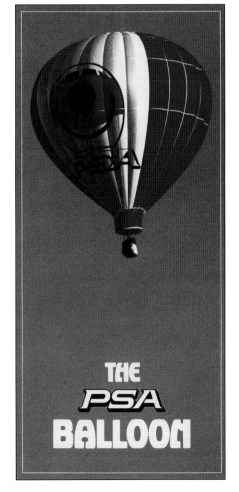

PSA used a hot-air balloon as a marketing tool for corporate accounts and travel agents. Adorned with the world-famous PSA smile, the balloon was a crowd-pleaser wherever it was flown.

In early 1985, PSA experimented with a new primer gray logo and paint scheme. Employees rejected it, and it was quickly withdrawn after only three aircraft had been repainted. (Photograph by Jay Selman.)

In early 1987, PSA showed off its final livery on this MD-80, which was purchased earlier from Air Cal.

This December 1987 photograph shows a PSA MD-80 landing at Phoenix after a quick flight from Los Angeles. PSA operated a total of 33 MD-80s, including two short-term leased aircraft from Hawaiian Air in the summer of 1985 due to delivery delays on the BAe146. (Photograph by Jay Selman.)

Five

PIEDMONT AIRLINES

In the summer of 1939, T.H. "Tom" Davis accepted a job from his former flying instructor, L.S. "Mac" McGinnis, to sell airplanes as Camel City Flying Service. On July 2, 1940, with funding in place, Camel ceased to exist, and a new company, Piedmont Aviation, Inc., was born, with Davis in charge. Davis's first motto was "Piedmont sets the pace." This would lead him to call all Piedmont aircraft "Pacemakers," a tradition that would last throughout the airline's history. With the United States drawn into World War II, and with Davis's outstanding reputation, Piedmont Aviation was able to train student pilots, including many from Allied countries in Central and South America. Davis's plan for starting service closely mirrored another new upstart airline, All American Aviation. On April 4, 1947, Piedmont was awarded route authority as a feeder airline in North Carolina and the Ohio River Valley, although Davis was surprised to learn that other airlines filed objections to this move.

On January 1, 1948, Davis created the airline division of Piedmont Aviation, called Piedmont Airlines. On February 20, 1948, Piedmont began operations with a six-stop service between Wilmington, North Carolina, and Cincinnati, Ohio. Piedmont officially rolled out its own paint scheme consisting of a white top, red and blue stripes running down the side of the aircraft, and the Piedmont speed bird located just aft of the passenger door. In 1955, Piedmont was awarded a permanent operating certificate by the CAB as a local service carrier. On June 6, 1956, Davis held a press conference stating that he was buying eight Fairchild F-27s, with delivery of the first aircraft in 1958. In the announcement, Fokker stated that Piedmont's specifications for a DC-3 replacement were largely responsible for Fokker teaming up with Fairchild in the United States to produce the F-27. In the spring of 1962, after much lobbying by Piedmont, including by Davis himself, authority was granted for several key south-to-north routes, which allowed Piedmont to link the cities with what had previously been predominately east-west routes. On February 20, 1963, Piedmont retired its last DC-3.

In January 1966, Davis flew to Seattle to sign a contract with Boeing for six 737-100s. Not long after the contract was signed, Boeing contacted Davis and the order was shifted to the slightly larger 737-200, which Davis felt was perfectly suited for Piedmont's route structure. Davis also penned an order for 10 Fairchild Hiller FH-227s. In March 1967, Davis flew to Japan to sign an order for 10 Japanese-built NAMC YS-11 turboprops. The first YS-11 was placed into scheduled service on May 19, 1968. In early April 1971, Piedmont's new Winston-Salem Reservation Center opened. In 1978, with deregulation, Piedmont immediately started conducting more nonstop flights while dropping smaller cities that could not support either the Boeing 737 or the YS-11 aircraft. Davis also flew to New York City to participate in a ceremony as Piedmont was added to the New York Stock Exchange.

In early 1981, Piedmont established Charlotte as the company's primary hub. On May 6, 1981, Tom Davis, who had guided Piedmont successfully for over four decades, announced his retirement from day-to-day operations, and he became chairman of the board. William Howard, who was one of the prominent vice presidents, was named president. In 1982, Piedmont signed on as a sponsor for NASCAR, and, on July 1 of that year, Dayton, Ohio, became the second hub for Piedmont. On July 15, 1983, Piedmont opened a third hub at Baltimore. The first two transcontinental flights using Boeing 727-200s took place on April 1, 1984, and inaugurated service from both Charlotte and Dayton to Los Angeles. In January 1985, Piedmont was named airline of the year by *Air Transport World*. On October 2, 1985, Howard announced that Piedmont was buying Utica, New York–based Empire Airlines. Later in October, after studying the Florida market for some time, Howard created the Piedmont Shuttle, operating to 10 Florida cities, with a dedicated fleet of nine F-28s operating 68 flights a day. In early 1986, pending route authority to London (Gatwick), Howard flew to Seattle to sign a six-plane order for new Boeing 767-200ERs. Piedmont was also the launch customer for the new Boeing 737-400.

On February 1, 1986, Piedmont completed the merger with Empire Airlines. In March 1987, after attempts were made to buy Piedmont by Norfolk & Western Railroad and Carl Icahn, US Air's Ed Colodny and Howard announced that Piedmont would merge with US Air. On June 15, 1987, Piedmont inaugurated transatlantic service with the Boeing 767. In August, Howard negotiated with Colodny to retire from Piedmont, and Bill McGee was named president and COO. On October 29, 1987, the Department of Transportation and the Department of Justice formally approved the merger. In June 1988, McGee resigned as president, and the board of directors named Tom Schick as his replacement. In 1989, because of the pending merger, the first few aircraft were delivered in the familiar Piedmont paint scheme, but the aircraft was polished aluminum versus a white body, making the conversion to US Air's paint scheme much easier. On August 5, 1989, Piedmont Airlines officially became US Air.

Piedmont's first group of 10 pilots stands proudly in front of the airline's first DC-3 in preparation for launching passenger flights. Shown here are, from left to right, Ed Clement, Milt Browning, John Wilkes, Ray Shulte, Zeke Saunders, Frank Nicholson, Hoss Dobbins, Leon Fox, Jack Tadlock, and Lee Cottrell.

On February 20, 1948, Piedmont Airlines took to the air for the first time, following the Civil Aeronautics Board's granting of a three-year temporary certificate. The first day of service involved a six-stop route between Wilmington, North Carolina, and Cincinnati, Ohio.

The first weekend after Piedmont began service, an open house was held in Wilmington to show off the "Pacemaker" DC-3.

In 1954, Pres. Tom Davis ordered the interiors of the DC-3s to be completely refurbished, including the installation of new, comfortable seats. Piedmont's reputation for safe, reliable, and friendly "Southern hospitality" service had helped the airline grow to a fleet of 16 DC-3s. This photograph shows the newly installed interior in early 1955.

Piedmont placed advertisements on billboards along highways. Myrtle Beach, which the airline started serving in 1949, was one of Piedmont's very popular cities, as seen on this advertisement in late 1955.

Piedmont's second Fairchild F-27 turboprop is shown flying over North Carolina during pilot training. November 14, 1958, marked the first day of service between Cincinnati and Wilmington. The large, oval windows, pressurization, and air-conditioning made the F-27 an instant favorite among passengers and crew.

When Davis found out that Trans World Airlines (TWA) was selling its Martin 404 fleet, Piedmont immediately bought all 17 aircraft for only $6.5 million. This would allow Davis to phase out the tired DC-3s that had faithfully served the airline. This Martin 404 is shown flying along the Carolina coast on March 15, 1962.

A couple celebrating their 60th anniversary step off a Piedmont F-27 in Asheville after flying in from Atlanta. Asheville station manager Jack Gwennap and stewardess Mary Bruney take a minute to congratulate the happy couple.

A Piedmont Martin 404 is shown boarding passengers in Charlotte for a quick flight to Winston-Salem in February 1963. With the entire fleet of Martin 404s entering service, Piedmont retired its last DC-3 on February 20, 1963. Many Piedmont employees came out to say goodbye to the Douglas aircraft that had faithfully served the company for over 15 years.

Piedmont's first Boeing 727-100 is shown flying over North Carolina in February 1967. Sadly, less than a month later, this Boeing 727 would be lost in an accident on takeoff from Asheville after being hit by a private plane.

During a cloudy morning in the spring of 1968, Piedmont's Fairchild Hiller FH-227 taxis out of Raleigh-Durham.

Piedmont's first Boeing 737-200 is shown undergoing pilot training over North Carolina in early May 1968. Davis had the aircraft initially configured with 94 seats in the five-across seating pattern rather than the standard six-across that other airlines were ordering. The Boeing twin-jet would begin scheduled service with Piedmont on May 30, 1968.

Piedmont's YS-11 is shown on February 15, 1971, preparing to take off from Jacksonville, North Carolina. Piedmont's first YS-11 began passenger service on May 19, 1968. Davis lowered the seating capacity to 58 and had an APU (auxiliary power unit) installed to make the aircraft interior temperature more comfortable on the ground when the engines were shut down. Davis also named the first YS-11 the *Cherry Blossom Pacemaker* to pay tribute to the Japanese-built aircraft.

This Piedmont Boeing 737 is shown landing at Washington, DC, in 1974, the same year that Piedmont rolled out a new paint scheme: a blue stripe, "Piedmont" in red lettering, and the speed bird proudly displayed on the tail. Clean and sharp, the design was an immediate hit with passengers and employees alike.

On October 25, 1975, Piedmont retired its last Fairchild Hiller FH-227, shown here sitting at the hangar after completing its last flight, ending nine years of service to many of Piedmont's smaller communities.

A Piedmont Boeing 727-100 is shown taxiing for a flight out of Washington National Airport in March 1980. Piedmont continued to purchase additional Boeing 727-100s and 737-200s as flights expanded following the passage of deregulation in 1978. (Photograph by Jay Selman.)

Piedmont employees are shown at the Atlanta ticket counter in April 1981. Piedmont employees were known as experts in customer service, and this enabled the company to grow as passengers flocked to the carrier.

On January 21, 1982, Tom Davis (right) accepted *Air Transport World*'s 1981 Marketing Development Award in New York City from 1980's recipient, US Air's Randall Malin.

On March 14, 1982, Piedmont retired its last YS-11 turboprop. The reliable Rolls-Royce Dart engine aircraft had served Piedmont for over 24 years. With the retirement of the YS-11s, Piedmont was now a pure jet carrier.

Piedmont's Charlotte hub is shown during a busy afternoon in April 1982. Piedmont opened a second hub in Dayton, Ohio, on July 1, 1982. Howard was buying used Boeing 727-200s while picking up additional new 737-200s.

On October 30, 1983, a Henson de Havilland Dash 7 is shown taxiing out of Baltimore as a feeder for Piedmont Airlines. Henson had originally been an Allegheny Commuter Airline for US Air, which was caught completely by surprise by Henson's move to become part of the Piedmont Commuter network. Henson would feed traffic at Piedmont's Baltimore hub with a fleet of Beech 99s and de Havilland Dash 7s. (Photograph by Jay Selman.)

A Piedmont Fokker F-28-1000 is shown conducting pilot training just prior to the April 1, 1984, inauguration of the aircraft. Piedmont was able to buy the entire fleet of Fokker F-28s from Garuda Indonesia.

Piedmont's first Boeing 737-300 aircraft was placed into service on May 1, 1985. Initially, the aircraft were delivered in an all-coach seating pattern for 138 passengers, but they would be reconfigured to 8 first-class and 120 coach seats when the planes were deployed on transcontinental routes.

A Piedmont Boeing 767 (in back) rests next to a regional airline's Brockway Saab 340 turboprop on the afternoon of April 16, 1986. Piedmont worked hard to support smaller communities that could not accommodate Piedmont's mainline aircraft. Piedmont penned agreements with other regional airlines, including Henson Airlines, Sunbird Airlines (which would become CC Air), Jetstream, and Britt Airways.

On June 15, 1987, Piedmont launched nonstop service from Charlotte to London (Gatwick) using new Boeing 767-200s. The City of Charlotte, the City of Tampa, and the Charlotte Douglas International Airport Authority were key in persuading the Department of Transportation to give Piedmont its first transatlantic destination. Piedmont's first Boeing 767, the *Pride of Piedmont*, would conduct the first flight.

Above, on February 20, 1988, as part of Piedmont's 40th anniversary of service, retired Piedmont founder Tom Davis (left) and its president, Bill McGee, pause in front of a refurbished DC-3 in Wilmington to thank the many loyal Piedmont employees. Davis was so beloved by the workers that, when he retired in 1981, they bought him a Mercedes-Benz.

As part of the celebration of the 40th anniversary of the company, retired pilots Leon Fox and Hoss Dobkins sit in the flight deck of the restored Piedmont DC-3. Fox and Dobkins piloted Piedmont's first flight on February 20, 1948.

A Piedmont Boeing 727-200 is shown landing in Charlotte after a transcontinental flight from San Francisco. (Photograph by Jay Selman.)

The fourth Boeing 767 of the six originally ordered sits in Charlotte in June 1988, with silver instead of the familiar white fuselage. After the announcement of the merger between Piedmont and US Air, Piedmont modified its paint scheme to speed up the transition of merging the two fleets.

A new Boeing 737-300 sits at Tampa in August 1988. Piedmont was already one of the largest operators of 737-300 aircraft. Following the US Air merger, the combined carrier would operate the world's largest fleet of Boeing 737-300s.

A Piedmont Fokker F-28-1000 taxis out of Charlotte for a flight to Florida in October 1988. Piedmont's F-28 fleet grew with the addition of the larger, 80-seat F-28-4000s. These were acquired as part of the merger with Empire Airlines on May 1, 1986. (Photograph by Jay Selman.)

Mike Cline, CC Air/Piedmont commuter station manager, and Kay Gilch, US Air manager of training records, show off the Piedmont/US Air merger T-shirts in the summer of 1988.

On September 15, 1988, Piedmont, operating as part of the US Air Group, received the first Boeing 737-400 aircraft. US Air's Ed Colodny ensured that respect was paid to Piedmont founder Tom Davis by having the first 737-400 named *Thomas H. Davis Pacemaker*.

Six

US Air

On October 28, 1979, Allegheny Airlines changed its name to US Air to reflect the company's growth from a regional carrier to a large-network, coast-to-coast airline. With deregulation less than two years old, company president Ed Colodny turned his attention to shifting from flights between short and medium markets to more long-haul flights between major metropolitan cities. He also sought to adjust times on existing flights to create hub-and-spoke networks at both Pittsburgh and Philadelphia. While other airlines were rapidly closing smaller cities, US Air was shifting flights to the Allegheny Commuter network, which had grown to 11 independent airlines and 75 aircraft serving communities throughout the Northeast. This provided direct passenger traffic feed to US Air, which gave the company an edge over other airlines serving the Northeast. Colodny flew to Seattle to sign a contract with Boeing for additional 727-200s, twenty 737-200s, and to be the colaunch customer for twenty 737-300s. Colodny later would fly to Long Beach to purchase additional McDonnell Douglas DC-9-30s.

During the first half of 1981, US Air continued to expand flights. Pittsburgh International Airport had completed work on a new passenger concourse, and this allowed US Air to offer that city as a major transfer point for travel. US Air also created a new program called Special Service Representatives. These specialized agents wore red coats and moved about the concourses, making themselves available to assist passengers in everything from providing connecting gate information to helping special passengers in transferring flights. US Air departures at Pittsburgh climbed to a record 191 flights a day to maximize passenger connections. In November, Allegheny Commuter marked its 15th anniversary. On March 15, 1983, US Air launched transcontinental routes from Pittsburgh to both San Francisco and Los Angeles with Boeing 727-200 aircraft.

In the first five years following deregulation, US Air added 25 cities in 11 different states and introduced a new frequent flyer program in February 1984. With US Air's continuing growth, Pittsburgh was now the nation's fifth-largest airline hub, with 267 daily departures. To improve customer service, US Air added computer technology that allowed passengers to reserve seat assignments up to three weeks in advance on both US Air and Allegheny Commuter flights. As 1986 began, airline mergers were happening at a rapid pace. Colodny started to look for an airline that could enhance US Air, and, with one phone call from Washington, DC, to PSA's president, Russell Ray, Colodny decided that acquiring PSA was exactly the shot in the arm that US Air needed. After both airlines' board of directors approved the sale, Colodny flew to San Diego to formally announce the merger and meet with frontline PSA employees. On March 6, 1987, Colodny and Piedmont's president, William Howard, held a joint press conference announcing that US Air would purchase Piedmont Airlines. On April 9, 1988, PSA was fully merged into US Air, and in June, US Air started retiring the BAC One-Elevens and found there was a very strong market for the aircraft. In September, the first Boeing 737-400 was received, which was part of the original Piedmont order. By spring 1989, after careful study, US Air started altering its all-coach fleet to include first-class seats. Allegheny Commuter's name was changed to US

Air Express on July 1, 1989, and, that same month, the first Fokker F-100 was delivered to US Air. The merger of US Air and Piedmont was completed on August 5.

Ed Colodny retired in 1990, and Seth Schofield succeeded him as CEO and president. In March 1992, US Air added the first Boeing 757 to the fleet. Schofield reached an agreement with Citicorp in April to operate the Trump Shuttle as the US Air Shuttle, using a fleet of Boeing 727-100s and 200s. In October, US Air moved into the state-of-the-art, midfield terminal at Pittsburgh, and in early 1993, it launched the US Air Florida Shuttle, offering point-to-point service. In 1995, US Air continued to build schedules at the hubs of Pittsburgh, Philadelphia, and Charlotte and expanded flights out of Washington National, Dulles, and Baltimore, while cutting service in California and abandoning the Florida shuttle market. Schofield retired from US Air, and the board of directors hired Stephen Wolf and Rakesh Gangwal. In early 1996, Wolf was named chairman and CEO of US Air, and in the spring, the company started new service from Philadelphia to Munich and Rome. Wolf knew that, in order to expand routes across the North Atlantic, he needed more wide-body aircraft.

Wolf announced in early 1997 that US Air would change its name to US Airways and adopt the tagline "Global Carrier of Choice." Wolf wanted to transition the airline from a domestic to an "international," world-class carrier. At a November 6 press conference, Wolf signed an order for 400 Airbus A-319/A-320/A-321 narrow-body aircraft. The name change to US Airways became official on February 1, 1997; at the end of the month, US Airways' last Fokker F-28 was retired, and the airline purchased the remaining interest in the US Airways Shuttle. After further negotiations with Airbus, an order was placed on July 2, 1998, for either 30 Airbus A-330 or Airbus A-340 wide-body aircraft. The first Airbus A-319 was delivered to US Airways on October 16, the first A-320 on January 29, 1999, and the first new A-330-300 wide-body on March 30, 2000.

On May 24, Gangwal announced that United Airlines would buy US Airways for $4.3 billion. The merger was complex, with immediate hurdles posed by labor unions, anti-trust regulations, and consumer groups. Meanwhile, on January 18, 2001, US Airways received the first Airbus A-321. Finally, on July 27, United withdrew the purchase offer to buy US Airways, as both companies knew that the Department of Transportation and the Department of Justice would never approve the merger.

The terrorist attacks of September 11 had an impact on all airlines but especially on US Airways. By the end of September, the company announced a large layoff affecting thousands of employees. As 2002 began, with US Airways still in deep financial trouble, David Siegel came aboard as president and CEO. Schedules and aircraft continued to be cut. On August 11, 2002, US Airways filed for Chapter 11 bankruptcy protection. In early 2004, Siegel turned his attention to markets where he felt US Airways could make money. Flights continued to be shifted from Pittsburgh to Philadelphia. In April, Siegel resigned from US Airways, and Bruce Lakefield, who was serving on the board of directors, was named president. Lakefield was forced to take the airline into bankruptcy for a second time on September 12, 2004. He made the difficult choice to de-hub Pittsburgh, with a major business change in mind. All international flights were moved from Pittsburgh to Philadelphia, along with other high-yield domestic cities.

In January 2005, as US Airways continued to suffer from a shrinking customer base and low morale, there was widespread speculation that the airline would shut down and be liquidated. This caught the attention of Tempe, Arizona–based America West, which was still reeling from the failed merger that Doug Parker had tried to arrange with American Trans Air in late 2004. Doug and his team flew to Crystal City to meet secretly with Lakefield and other leaders of US Airways. By March, "Project Barbell" was under way. Project Barbell got its name from the east route system of US Airways and the west route system of America West. Speculation of a merger began soon after. US Airways received permission to use "restricted" cash to continue operations, and both companies denied rumors that a merger was forthcoming. Working with confidentiality clauses from both airlines, Parker and Lakefield received the green light from both boards of directors, and by early May, the deal was done.

With the name change to US Air on October 28, 1979, the company's president, Ed Colodny, acquired 11 Boeing 727-100s from United Airlines, allowing him to expand to the Midwest and the West Coast.

During the summer of 1980, US Air started stripping the white paint off the aircraft and instead polished the fuselage, which saved on fuel and lowered maintenance costs. The new look can be seen on this Boeing 727-200 flying over Pennsylvania on August 1, 1981.

US Air employees model new uniforms in front of a DC-9-30 at Pittsburgh. The uniform presented a crisp and professional image.

On November 1, 1982, US Air placed its first Boeing 737-200 into service. That first 737 is shown here on a morning flight between Pittsburgh and Philadelphia on May 15, 1983.

On July 20, 1983, a DC-9-30 taxis for a flight out of Allentown and a quick hop to Pittsburgh. US Air would fly a total of 75 DC-9s.

US Air president Ed Colodny is shown at Boeing headquarters in December 1984 accepting delivery of the first 737-300. US Air and Southwest Airlines were the launch customers for the updated version of the 737.

US Air's second Boeing 737-300 is shown over Seattle undergoing its delivery test flight. The first day of service for this CFM-powered aircraft was December 18, 1984. At the end of 1984, US Air had 125 aircraft conducting over 1,000 flights a day to 70 cities across the United States and Canada.

This British-built BAC One-Eleven is shown taxiing out of Dayton on May 1, 1985. That same month, Colodny flew to the Netherlands to buy new Fokker F-100s meant to replace the aging twin-jet.

This January 1986 photograph shows US Air's ticket counter at Pittsburgh, which was the nation's fifth-largest airline hub, with over 267 daily departures.

On September 1, 1987, in Pittsburgh, a Detroit-bound DC-9-30 taxis by an Allegheny Commuter Shorts 330 and three de Havilland Twin Otters. Colodny sought to extend reliable air service to smaller communities that could not accommodate the larger jet aircraft.

On April 8, 1988, PSA became US Air, and with the merger, US Air inherited 30 MD-80s, 4 DC-9-30s, and 22 BAe146-200s. The day after the completion of the merger, this BAe146 is pictured taxiing out of terminal one at Los Angeles for a flight to Fresno.

US Air's Pittsburgh hub is shown full of aircraft during an afternoon "bank" of flights on March 5, 1989. Following US Air's merger of PSA, Colodny focused his attention on working with Piedmont's president, William Howard, to complete the merger of Piedmont and US Air.

On May 24, 1989, Colodny rolled out a new paint scheme to celebrate the upcoming merger with Piedmont. A polished fuselage was maintained, and a large red stripe and a narrow blue stripe ran the length of the fuselage. The tail was blue, and "US Air" was written on the fuselage in red and Piedmont blue. This US Air MD-80, taxiing out of Tampa for Pittsburgh, shows the updated paint scheme.

On July 1, 1989, Allegheny Commuter became US Air Express. The change is reflected on a Shorts 330 (in the background) and US Air Boeing 737-200, shown here in Philadelphia. Less than one year later, Ed Colodny would retire after having faithfully served the airline since 1957.

A US Air Boeing 727-200 is shown taxiing out of Washington National Airport during the summer of 1992. US Air would retire the reliable tri-jet in December 1992, although 727s would continue to operate the former Trump Shuttle routes as the US Air Shuttle.

Not all of the Fokker F-28s inherited from the merger with Piedmont were stripped of paint and polished. US Air chose to paint some of the F-28s gray, as illustrated by this former Empire Airlines Fokker F-28-4000, pictured in Orlando on a spring day in 1993.

A Boeing 737-400 flies over the Rocky Mountains during a transcontinental flight from Los Angeles to Pittsburgh on April 2, 1994. This 737-400 was one of 54 ordered by US Air, making the carrier the world's largest operator of both the Boeing 737-300 and 737-400.

A US Air Boeing 757-200 is shown landing at Los Angeles on October 12, 1995. US Air's Boeing 757s were made up of a combination of former Eastern models and new aircraft ordered directly from Boeing.

After flying across the Atlantic from Frankfurt, this Boeing 767-200 is shown landing in Pittsburgh on November 30, 1995.

This Fokker F-100 in Charlotte is taking off for a flight to Atlanta during the afternoon of April 2, 1996. The F-100 was just the right aircraft for US Air's thinner routes and off-peak flights.

Shown just as it is rotating off the runway at Charlotte, this US Air Boeing 737-300 heads to Boston during the spring of 1997. Around this time, Stephen Wolf announced that the carrier would become US Airways. A more conservative paint scheme was adopted, consisting of a gray bottom, a midnight blue top, and a stylized flag on the tail.

A DC-9-30 takes off from Charlotte bound for Kansas City on a fall morning in 1997. On November 6, Wolf would announce the largest aircraft order in the history of the United States, which called for the purchase of 400 Airbus A-319s, A-320s, and A-321s.

Wolf continued to push for more international expansion across the Atlantic. This included new nonstop service from Philadelphia to Manchester, England, which was initially achieved with Boeing 767s.

On October 16, 1998, Wolf (center) was in Toulouse, France, with a group of employees picking up the first Airbus A-319.

Wolf holds a press conference in Philadelphia to show off the new Airbus A-320. US Airways' first A-320 was delivered on January 29, 1999.

A US Airways Boeing 757 undergoes de-icing at Baltimore on a winter day in 1999.

On January 18, 2001, US Airways received the first Airbus A-321. Older Boeing aircraft were being retired at an accelerated rate.

The world of aviation changed forever on September 11, 2001. With its hub at Washington National shut down for months, US Airways quickly became one of the most vulnerable airlines. This US Airways Fokker F-100, one of the few with the new paint scheme, is seen shortly before the fleet was retired in December 2002.

On May 4, 2004, US Airways joined the Star Alliance network. This agreement was very important to the airline, opening up additional markets to transfer passengers. A Boeing 737-300 is seen here taxiing out of Fort Lauderdale, which US Airways' president, Bruce Lakefield, beefed up as a focus hub city.

Seven

AMERICA WEST AIRLINES

Ed Beauvais, having worked for airlines including Frontier, Bonanza, and Air West, as well as having operated his own aviation consulting firm, decided in 1981 that Phoenix was the perfect place to start an airline. Its geographic relationship to the West Coast, mild climate, abundant airport gates, and uncongested airspace made it a diamond in the desert. On September 4, 1981, America West was incorporated, and Beauvais focused on raising enough startup capital through an IPO to ride out the typical peaks and valleys that occur when a new company begins service.

On August 1, 1983, with 277 employees and three Boeing 737-200s, America West began service from Phoenix to Kansas City, Wichita, Colorado Springs, and Los Angeles. In July 1985, America West became a feeder for Northwest Orient while establishing an air cargo division to take advantage of the strong demand for reliable shipping. In 1987, with the merger of Republic Airlines and Northwest, Beauvais was able to pick up six Rolls-Royce-powered Boeing 757s that he immediately deployed to Chicago and the East Coast cities of Baltimore and New York (Kennedy), and introduced 14-seat "business class." Beauvais would also open the first Phoenix Club airport lounge at Phoenix, while a second reservation center would open in Reno. Because of the aggressive growth, Ansett Airlines of Australia invested 10 percent in America West, giving the company a much-needed capital infusion. In February 1988, America West opened its own hangar and technical support center, which included a state-of-the-art stripping and painting facility. Operation Freedom Bird was also started, a program that provided Vietnam veterans with transportation to the Vietnam Veterans Memorial in Washington, DC.

In early 1989, Beauvais wanted America West to grow beyond the continental United States. He started applying for international destinations and kept in mind that frequent flyers enrolled in America West's Flight Fund program wanted Hawaii as one option with which to redeem their credits. America West applied for but was denied by the Department of Transportation to begin service to Tokyo and Sydney but, on a subsequent attempt, was awarded Nagoya, Japan. After a worldwide search for wide-body aircraft, Beauvais was able to buy four used Boeing 747-200s from KLM Royal Dutch Airlines, and he penned an order for four new Boeing 747-400s. In November 1989, America West launched its Boeing 747 "Bird of Paradise" service to Honolulu from both Phoenix and Las Vegas. In 1990, America West acquired 16 Airbus A-320s, and on February 1, 1991, it launched service to Nagoya. Meanwhile, however, in an attempt to stimulate travel and raise cash, a 50-percent-off ticket sale was held. On June 27, 1991, America West filed for bankruptcy. Immediately, 13 cities were closed, aircraft were parked, and the Nagoya route was sold to Northwest Airlines, while employees and executives took pay cuts to stabilize the company.

In December 1991, America West opened a mini-hub in Columbus, Ohio. The company started to develop service to key cities in Mexico the following year, while the Dash 8s were parked as service to smaller cities was turned over to Mesa Airlines, which was now a code-share partner, and founder Ed Beauvais stepped down as chairman. America West emerged from bankruptcy on August 26, 1994. The reorganization was accomplished via three main sources of assistance: Texas Pacific Group, Mesa Airlines, and Continental Airlines, who started a comprehensive code share with America West. The company became the official airline of the Arizona Diamondbacks in 1995, and two years later, it formed America West Holdings, creating separate divisions for America West and the Leisure Company, which was a rebrand of America West vacations. Meanwhile, Phoenix Reservations moved to a new location. At year's end, America West was awarded J.D. Power and Associates' award for flights less than 500 miles. In 1999, the airline's corporate headquarters was relocated to a new nine-story building in Tempe. Doug Parker was named chairman, CEO, and president of America West on the first day of September, 2001. Only 10 days later, he would face the challenge of his career when the United States was attacked by terrorists. America West, like all airlines, faced a dramatic drop in air travel, and it received a $429-million loan from the federal government to keep from going out of business.

In 2002, America West revamped all of its air fares, causing Continental to drop the code-share arrangement. That same year, a new operations and training center was opened. As demand for air travel rebounded, America West rolled out new tray-table advertising for all aircraft in 2003, and the following year, it began "Buy on Board" meal service for coach passengers. In November 2004, Parker worked hard to try to merge with American Trans Air (ATA); however, ATA would file for bankruptcy, and a deal was instead worked out with Southwest Airlines, leaving Parker on the sidelines. In early 2005, rumors began circulating that America West was working on a potential merger with US Airways. Internally, Parker and his executives were working on the merger, called "Operation Barbell," based on America West's and US Airways' strong presence on the West and the East Coasts. On May 18, 2005, Parker and US Airways' Bruce Lakefield jointly announced the merger. America West's operating certificate was dissolved as the merger was completed on September 26, 2007. Despite this, Ed Beauvais's dream of making air travel affordable had been realized, and he played a large role in economic development in Phoenix and all of Arizona. Beauvais succeeded in shaping not only an airline but an industry.

Shown here on a McDonnell Douglas DC-9-30 is the proposed paint scheme for America West when Ed Beauvais officially created the airline on September 4, 1981. (Courtesy of Ed and Mary Ellen Beauvais.)

In 1983, a second paint scheme was proposed, but it also was not implemented. (Courtesy of Ed and Mary Ellen Beauvais.)

Beauvais's sister-in-law, Evelyn Daurio, came up with the name "America West." Shown here is the final adopted paint scheme. The first three Boeing 737-200s were leased by Guinness Peat Aviation, with the aircraft coming from Pacific Western of Canada. (Courtesy of Ed and Mary Ellen Beauvais.)

Ed and Mary Ellen Beauvais proudly stand in front of many of the original 277 employees and the company's first Boeing 737-200. It was very important to the Beauvaises to give the new airline a "family feel," which contributed to the explosive growth of the new airline. (Courtesy of Ed and Mary Ellen Beauvais.)

Beauvais made sure that America West would stand out from the crowd. All America West employees bought stock in the company, and all passengers received complimentary cocktails and the *Wall Street Journal* on all flights. This photograph, taken on October 15, 1983, shows a billboard at the west entrance of Sky Harbor International Airport.

By January 1984, America West's fleet had grown to 10 Boeing 737-200s. At the company's one-year anniversary, the airline had doubled its size, capturing an impressive 21 percent of the Phoenix market and operating to 23 cities. America West increased its gates from three to nine to support its growth. This photograph from August 1, 1984, shows terminal three.

America West's first Boeing 737-300 is shown undergoing final flight tests over Seattle, with Mount Rainier visible above the clouds. America West would put the 737-300 into service in February 1985.

In February 1986, America West entered into an agreement with Greyhound to provide bus service between Phoenix Sky Harbor and Scottsdale (service to Mesa would be discontinued due to low passenger loads). The bus routes were listed in the system as flights, and passengers could board the "Careliner" bus directly from a gate, as shown here in April 1986.

In September 1987, America West's vice president of sales, Tom Burns (far left), and Beauvais entertain corporate guests and travel agents at the grand opening of the first Phoenix Club at terminal three. Beauvais's wife, Mary Ellen, had personally decorated the club with tasteful Southwest flare. (Courtesy of Ed and Mary Ellen Beauvais.)

In December 1988, America West was awarded the number one airline, having achieved the best on-time performance of the year for all US-based airlines, by the Department of Transportation. To showcase this incredible feat, Daphne Dicino, manager of corporate communications, worked with the marketing department to gather as many employees as she could from the various departments for a photograph, which was then made into posters, billboards, and advertisements.

In early 1987, with smaller cities in Arizona requesting air service, Beauvais penned an order for the de Havilland Dash 8. The 37-seat turboprop aircraft was perfect for smaller markets that could not support the larger jets. This Dash 8 was photographed near the Grand Canyon on April 5, 1989.

One of America West's Boeing 737-200s is shown landing in Phoenix on July 1, 1989. America West would eventually operate 71 Boeing 737-200s.

On November 30, 1989, this America West Boeing 747 takes off from Honolulu for its transpacific return flight to Phoenix.

An America West Boeing 757 sits at Phoenix on the evening of April 20, 1990. America West received this 757 from Boeing new in October 1989.

In 1990, America West became the official carrier of the Phoenix Suns professional basketball team. To celebrate, the airline added a special Phoenix Suns logo to the sole remaining Boeing 737-100, shown taxiing out of Phoenix on January 5, 1991.

Troops returning from the Gulf War board one of the Boeing 747s, decorated with the words "Freedom Bird" and a yellow ribbon to welcome them home.

Below, an America West Airbus A-320 flies over Kansas City in the winter of 1993. America West would become an important customer to Airbus and would eventually operate 67 A-320s.

The author and his wife, Terri Mango-Lehman, stand in the first-class cabin of a Boeing 757 on January 1, 1994. America West picked up this 757, along with four others, from Eastern Airlines.

The word "Arizona" and that state's flag are proudly displayed on this Boeing 757 taxiing at Phoenix on July 4, 1994. America West would paint two other state flags on 757s honoring Nevada and Ohio, the airline's two other hubs.

In February 1996, the airline's chairman, Bill Franke, rolled out America West's new corporate identity, which included a revised logo with red and teal as the primary colors. The new scheme is displayed on this Boeing 737-300 taxiing out of Phoenix on February 28, 1996. (Photograph by Capt. Steve Gay.)

America West took delivery of the company's first Airbus A-319 on November 1, 1998. America West would operate a fleet of 39 of the smaller Airbus by 2005. (Photograph by Capt. Steve Gay.)

Mesa Airlines became an express carrier for America West in late 1992 and would adopt the new paint scheme, as illustrated on this CRJ-200 departing for Eugene on October 1, 2004.

Numerous America West aircraft sit during the afternoon bank at the company's Phoenix hub on December 12, 2004, shortly after the collapse of merger talks with American Trans Air.

On January 19, 2005, America West retired its last Boeing 737-200. Its final flight was from Ontario to Phoenix. Doug Parker held a decommissioning ceremony the next day.

An America West Boeing 757 taxis to the gate at Phoenix after arriving from Maui on February 20, 2005. The Boeing 757 would also fly to Honolulu, Kauai, and Hawaii.

An America West Airbus A-320 takes off from Fort Lauderdale for Phoenix on May 18, 2005. (Photograph by Capt. Steve Gay).

Eight

EMPIRE AIRLINES

On September 22, 1975, Paul Quakenbush, believing that Utica could support a second passenger airline, launched Oneida County Aviation, which used a Piper Aztec between Utica and Syracuse. The success of the route spurred Quakenbush to split the company into two parts, one for flying airplanes, the other a new airline called Empire. By mid-1976, Empire phased out the Piper Aztec and in its place added a Piper Navajo. In the fall, Quakenbush flew to San Antonio to sign an order for five Fairchild Swearingen Metroliner IIs, with first delivery planned for mid-1977. Empire's first Metroliner began passenger service in June of that year. Allegheny Airlines was retreating from several markets in May 1978, and Empire moved to add service in those cities. On July 1, 1979, Empire became the first certified commuter airline in the country, and, later in the year, Quakenbush flew to the Netherlands to sign a purchase order for the 80-seat Fokker F-28-4000, the first of which was delivered on August 1, 1980. In November 1982, Quakenbush signed a comprehensive marketing and code-share agreement with Pan Am called the "Empire–Pan Am Express;" it was the perfect fit for both airlines, as Empire was already using Pan Am's gates at New York–Kennedy's Worldport terminal. The agreement would allow Empire passengers to connect to Pan Am's extensive worldwide network, while Pan Am would use Empire to connect international passengers to western and central New York.

In August 1984, Empire added its first two international destinations, Montreal and Ottawa, from Syracuse, which had become the airline's major hub city. Empire, named *Air Transport World*'s regional airline of the year for 1984, had become the second-largest regional carrier in the United States, serving 22 cities with a fleet of Swearingen Metroliners and Fokker F-28s. In September, Quakenbush announced plans to phase out the Metroliners by the end of the year to focus the company on being a pure jet carrier. As Empire's stock started spiking upward, rumors started floating around in December that many large airlines were courting Quakenbush. One month later, Piedmont Airlines offered to buy Empire for $40 million. With no route duplication between the two carriers, and Piedmont's desire to pick up a significant amount of Northeast routes, it was the perfect marriage for the two companies. In addition, Piedmont, like Empire, was aggressively buying Fokker F-28s from all over the world.

In January 1986, Empire shareholders voted in favor of the merger. Piedmont in turn promised that no Empire employees would be laid off or lose their job because of the merger. Quakenbush was offered a vice president position at Piedmont, but he instead negotiated an agreement that he would retain exclusive rights to the Empire name. Quakenbush left the airline and began work on building a boat line named Empire near Thousand Oaks, New York. On May 1, 1986, Empire became Piedmont. Tragically, Paul Quakenbush, regarded as a visionary, died in an automobile accident in 1991.

Pictured at Washington National in February 1980 is Empire's third Piper Navajo, which the company's president, Paul Quakenbush, placed into service in late 1977. (Photograph by Jay Selman.)

Sitting between flights at Washington National on December 5, 1980, is the last Piper Navajo purchased by Quakenbush. Empire would phase out all of the Navajos by December 31, 1980. (Photograph by Jay Selman.)

Empire's fifth Swearingen Metroliner II is shown at Washington National in September 1981. The airline's new paint scheme was introduced with the delivery of the first Metroliner. (Photograph by Jay Selman.)

Quakenbush, with the support of the pilots, pushed his airline to the next level with the Fokker F-28-4000, which was introduced on September 15, 1980. The aircraft shown here, sitting at Syracuse in July 1982, was Empire's fourth F-28. (Photograph by Jay Selman.)

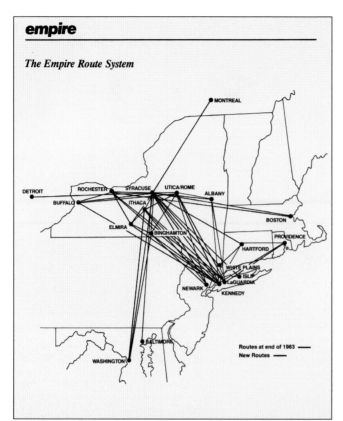

empire

The Empire Route System

MONTREAL

DETROIT
ROCHESTER · SYRACUSE · UTICA/ROME · ALBANY
BUFFALO · ITHACA
ELMIRA · BINGHAMTON
BOSTON
PROVIDENCE
HARTFORD
WHITE PLAINS · ISLIP
NEWARK · LaGUARDIA
KENNEDY
BALTIMORE
WASHINGTON

Routes at end of 1983 ——
New Routes ——

Here is Empire's route map in 1983. As 1984 opened, Empire continued to add service in key East Coast cities to continue to dominate the Northeast.

A pair of Empire Fokker F-28s shares the ramp with a Pan Am Boeing 727-200 at Pan Am's Worldport terminal at New York–Kennedy during a warm spring afternoon in 1983.

Above, Empire's Syracuse hub is busy during the afternoon of July 5, 1984. The airline was named *Air Transport World*'s Regional Airline of the Year in 1984.

PIEDMONT AIRLINES

System Schedule Effective January 15, 1986.

empire

THE NEW AIR FORCE IN THE NORTHEAST.

With the merger approved, Piedmont and Empire issued their first joint timetable on January 15, 1986. Piedmont coveted Empire's strength in the Northeast and its fleet of larger Fokker F-28s.

Shown between flights at Newark in February 1986 is Empire's F-28 in a hybrid merger paint scheme. The shareholders of both airlines overwhelmingly agreed to the sale of Empire to Piedmont.

Piedmont ramp agents John Szpyrka (left) and Marty Goldwych (right) are shown walking away from one Empire F-28 that is departing while the other has just deplaned passengers during a cold morning in February 1986.

Nine

TRUMP SHUTTLE

In March 1989, Texas Air Corporation's Frank Lorenzo bought Eastern Airlines, which included the Eastern Shuttle. The shuttle could trace its origin to April 30, 1961, when it began service between Washington, DC, New York (LaGuardia), and Boston. Not long after acquiring Eastern, Lorenzo placed the Eastern Shuttle on the auction block. High-profile businessman Donald Trump came forward with the highest offer, financed through 22 banks and a $380-million loan. When Trump bought the shuttle, he stated that one of the airline's biggest assets was the employees, especially the flight attendants. One such flight attendant was Bette Burke-Nash, who had been at Eastern for only four years when the shuttle started. Although Burke-Nash had the option of working mainline Eastern Airlines flights, she chose the shuttle. She and other flight attendants knew the passengers and their families by name, something Trump not only recognized but felt would continue to give his airline an important advantage over the rival Pan Am Shuttle.

On June 7, 1989, the Trump Shuttle was born. Trump immediately refurbished the interiors of the former Eastern Boeing 727s by adding maple wood veneer, chrome seat belts, and gold lavatory fixtures. The fleet was painted with red, gold, and black stripes and a large "T" on the tail. The Trump Shuttle was an early leader in check-in technologies, including, at LaGuardia, the first passenger kiosks that allowed complete self-check-in. Trump also partnered with LapStop, a new company that rented laptops to passengers. All of the upgrades of the airport and aircraft were done in light of Trump's marketing his shuttle as a luxury service. He thought this would bring back customers who had defected to the Pan Am Shuttle or Amtrak's Metroliner train service. Trump was wrong—passengers were only interested in the price of the ticket. This factor, combined with an economic recession and the doubling of jet fuel prices due to the Gulf War, placed enormous pressure on the Trump Shuttle.

On September 1, 1990, the Trump Shuttle defaulted on its loan, and the lead bank, Citicorp, took control as ownership reverted to the banks. US Air approached the banks and successfully negotiated an extremely complex arrangement whereby US Air Group (the holding company of US Air) would take over and assume 40-percent ownership and would run the shuttle for 10 years. On April 12, 1992, the Trump Shuttle became the US Air Shuttle. US Airways purchased the remaining 60 percent of the shuttle on November 19, 1997, and continued to operate the US Airways Shuttle separately from the rest of the airline. In May 1999, the first Airbus A-320 was delivered and placed into the US Airways Shuttle fleet; the decision had been made to start retiring all of the Boeing 727s. On July 1, 2000, the US Airways Shuttle was merged into the airline's mainline fleet. By December 2000, the US Airways Shuttle had a dedicated fleet of nine Airbus A-319s and eight Airbus A-320s. After the merger with America West in 2005, US Airways ceased dedicating aircraft specifically to the shuttle, although today most of the shuttle flights are operated with Embraer E-190s, which US Airways purchased new from Embraer in December 2006.

Shown shortly after Donald Trump bought the Eastern Shuttle on June 7, 1989, is one of Trump Shuttle's Boeing 727-100s, still in Eastern colors. (Photograph by Ron Peel.)

Sitting between shuttle flights on March 14, 1990, is one of Trump Shuttle's Boeing 727-100s. (Photograph by Ron Peel.)

This 1990 Trump Shuttle advertisement was given to travel agents and corporate accounts to promote the airline. Trump would spend millions of dollars advertising his "premier" airline.

This Trump Boeing 727-200 sits at LaGuardia on September 1, 1990. On the same day, the Trump Shuttle defaulted on the loan given to Trump, and control of the company reverted to the banks. (Photograph by Ron Peel.)

Shown landing at Washington National from LaGuardia in October 1994 is this US Air Shuttle Boeing 727-200. US Air assumed a 40-percent stake in the company and would buy the remaining 60 percent on November 19, 1997. (Photograph by Jay Selman.)

This US Air DC-9-30 is shown at LaGuardia in November 1999. To help speed the retirement of the Boeing 727s, US Air temporarily moved five DC-9-30s and a few Boeing 737-300s in the summer and fall of 1999. (Photograph by Jay Selman.)

Taken on October 21, 2000, this photograph shows US Airways Shuttle's last Boeing 727-200 taxiing out of LaGuardia as the fleet was retired. (Photograph by Joe McCarthy.)

Flight attendant Bette Burke-Nash (center) is shown with two unidentified fellow flight attendants at Washington National. Betty is currently the number-one flight attendant at US Airways and proudly continues to work the shuttle flights. Betty has worked on the shuttle for so many years that, in many cases, she knows three generations of the same family.

For a period of time, nine Airbus A-319s and eight A-320s were used exclusively on the shuttle, including this A-320. (Photograph by Jay Selman.)

Ten

METROJET

In 1997, US Airways president Rakesh Gangwal assembled a team of employees from every part of the airline to determine if the company should start a low-fare airline. US Airways Labor Relations met with unionized employees to negotiate increased productivity and flexibility to achieve a lower cost-per-seat-mile. This was required in order to start a new airline within an airline. Early on, the decision was made to feature only one aircraft type, and to utilize an all-coach configuration. The Boeing 737-200 was picked, since the aircraft was already in abundance.

In January 1998, the name "MetroJet" was chosen from a number of names submitted by employees. Michael Scherringa was tapped to head MetroJet, and he, along with his team, decided that Baltimore would be the home base for the new airline. While many flights would pass thorough Baltimore, a point-to-point network would be established to fly from the Northeast and Midwest to Florida, maintaining a focus on vacation destinations. On June 1, 1998, MetroJet launched service from Baltimore to Cleveland, Fort Lauderdale, Providence, and Manchester, New Hampshire. By the end of the year, more Boeing 737-200s were transferred to MetroJet from mainline US Airways.

In January 1999, MetroJet added additional point-to-point service from the Northeast corridor to various cities in Florida. By early 2000, MetroJet was flying 46 Boeing 737-200s, offering 182 daily flights as far west as Chicago (Midway) and New Orleans, while continuing to shuffle traffic from the Northeast to Florida. In early 2001, although MetroJet was achieving high load factors, it was not making money. Since Scherringa could not ask for more productivity from the employees, he considered switching to newer aircraft, including MD-80s, Fokker F-100s, or Boeing 737-300s. With the attacks of September 11, all plans to change the strategy of MetroJet ended. On September 26, 2001, Gangwal announced that MetroJet would cease operations by December. The final MetroJet flight was parked at Baltimore in December 2001 as the little red airline flew into the sunset.

The president of US Airways, Rakesh Gangwal, is shown at a press conference in January 1998 announcing the formation of MetroJet.

One of MetroJet's Boeing 737-200s is shown at Baltimore just prior to the launch of service on June 1, 1998. MetroJet 737s were painted red on top and gray on the belly and retained the US Airways navy tail.

On June 1, 1998, passengers are lined up outside of Baltimore International to receive "goodie bags" as they wait to check in for the first flight of MetroJet.

Two actors dressed as Abraham Lincoln and George Washington greet passengers as they prepare to board the first MetroJet flight.

Gate agents at Baltimore prepare to board MetroJet's first flight on June 1, 1998.

MetroJet's first Boeing 737 taxis out of the gate at Baltimore toward the runway while receiving a water-cannon salute.

This MetroJet aircraft sits idle at Baltimore in December 2001, just after the last MetroJet flight was shut down.

Eleven

NEW US AIRWAYS

On May 18, 2005, America West's chairman of the board, Doug Parker, and US Airways' chairman of the board, Bruce Lakefield, held a press conference in Tempe to announce the merger of US Airways and America West. Following the approvals of shareholders, both airlines' board of directors, the Department of Transportation, and the Department of Justice, the merger of the two holding companies was completed on September 27, 2005. On August 23, 2005, an Airbus A-320 modeling the new US Airways paint scheme completed a transcontinental road show that also highlighted the release of the heritage logo and the throwback liveries of Allegheny, America West, Piedmont, and PSA that would be painted on Airbus A-319s by mid-2006. Elise Eberwein, who at the time was senior vice president of culture, people, and corporate communications, declared as a top priority open and honest communication with employees. This was achieved through weekly employee newsletters and frequent face-to-face meetings between executives and employees. Her strategy of frank and open communication continuies today and pay dividends.

On September 27, 2007, US Airways was awarded a single operating certificate. By the end of 2008, US Airways had added "heritage display cases" throughout key buildings around the country and painted some aircraft in NFL themes representing the Philadelphia Eagles, Pittsburgh Steelers, Carolina Panthers, and Arizona Cardinals. On January 15, 2009, US Airways flight 1549 ditched into the Hudson River after hitting a flock of geese. A special ceremony was held in Charlotte on February 27 to honor the crew and passengers. In May, US Airways would take delivery of the Airbus A-330-200 while placing orders for the Airbus A-350. US Airways, a company built on tradition, played a very important role in the development of air transportation. In the early years of deregulation, US Air, now known as US Airways, set the pace for the industry and, in the 21st century, it continues to be a trendsetter. Its family of more than 32,000 employees looks at the past with respect while looking with anticipation to the future of the great airline.

On August 23, 2005, US Airways' first aircraft painted in the new livery taxis to the hangar at Phoenix after completing a transcontinental rollout at Philadelphia, Pittsburgh, Charlotte, Las Vegas, and Phoenix.

US Airways' Bruce Lakefield (right) and America West's Doug Parker (left) introduce the new US Airways paint scheme to employees on August 23, 2005.

Three airline "legends"—Ed Beauvais (left), Doug Parker (center), and Ed Colodny—pose for pictures at the dedication of the new corporate headquarters "Heritage Lobby" on September 26, 2006.